Psychic Development

3 Easy Steps To Developing Your Intuition

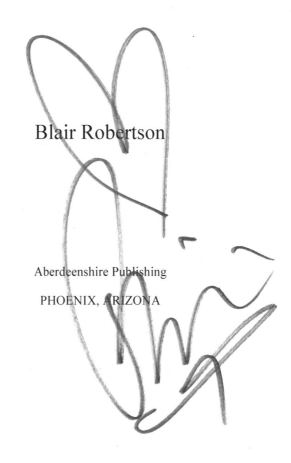

Blair Robertson

Aberdeenshire Publishing

PHOENIX, ARIZONA

Copyright © 2015 by **Blair Robertson**

All rights reserved. No part of this publication may be reproduced, distributed or transmitted in any form or by any means, without prior written permission.

Aberdeenshire Publishing
Box 1306
Litchfield Park, Arizona 85340

The information presented herein represents the view of the author as of the date of publication. Because of the rate with which conditions change, the author reserves the right to alter and update his opinion based on the new conditions. This is for informational purposes only. While every attempt has been made to verify the information provided in this report, neither the author nor his affiliates/partners assume any responsibility for errors, inaccuracies or omissions. Any slights of people or organizations are unintentional. If advice concerning legal or related matters is needed, the services of a fully qualified professional should be sought. Contents are not intended for use as a source of legal or accounting advice. You should be aware of any laws that govern business transactions or other business practices in your country and state. Any reference to any person or business whether living or dead is purely coincidental. Hug an attorney today.

ISBN-13: 978-1507756539

ISBN-10: 1507756534

Psychic Development: 3 Steps To Developing Your Psychic Intuition/ Blair Robertson. -- 1st ed.

To Dr. Spencer P. Thornton
For having the vision to give others vision

"The psychic world is like electricity—both exist whether you believe in them or not."

—EDDIE DIIJON

Table of Contents

Welcome!

Hi, I'm Blair Robertson, and I'd like to thank you very much for buying my book.

The purpose of this book is simple: to help you develop your intuitive abilities, which will in turn help you improve your business and personal life.

I'm best known today as a psychic medium, but in the late 1990s and early 2000s, I worked as a professional stage hypnotist and psychic. I also presented a popular three-hour seminar called "The Intuitive Edge" to colleges, universities, and high schools. This presentation covered—in a fun way—the basics of psychic development.

Back then, like today, students had short attention spans, so my presentation was designed to quickly demonstrate intuition that students could put into practice immediately.

This book is based on that. It's basic, it's quick, and it's easy.

One of the most popular gifts in the 'psychic biz' is tarot cards. Tarot cards are awesome. The problem is that there are seventy-eight cards, and you must deeply learn the meanings of each card before you can start. Then you need to know and completely understand a card layout (called a spread). This requires considerable practice before you can even start to be good at it.

As much as I love the tarot cards, I feel they are too steep of a curve for beginners.

But a pendulum, which we'll explore soon, can be learned in minutes. I've taught 7-year old kids how to use one. A pendulum is quick, easy, and very rewarding.

By the end of the book, you'll have that and several other tools you can use in your daily life to gain help from the spiritual realm, gain insight into your future, and be able to read others.

Also, for the first time, I will reveal how I have made some of my astonishing predictions, such as the Japanese earthquake and tsunami, using what I call "Time Projected Empathy."

If you master Time Projected Empathy, you too could be predicting the future!

I sincerely hope you enjoy this book as much as I have enjoyed writing it! Now let's talk about psychic intuition.

What is Psychic Intuition?

Without getting too deep in "woo-woo" definitions, let me give you an overview of what psychic intuition is and is not.

One of the biggest misconceptions is the so-called sixth sense. There's no such thing as a sixth sense. We only have five senses. We can see, hear, smell, feel, and taste.

What spirit does is heighten our senses and connect to us in that manner. We'll discuss more about those heightened senses – the "clairs" – in an upcoming chapter.

A good way to look at it is this: We are spiritual people living in a physical body. We are all connected in a spiritual manner. Once we understand that we're not limited by our physical bodies or physical limitations, we are free to tap into the higher power.

A once-popular term for tapping into that higher power was ESP, or Extra Sensory Perception. I prefer to call it Enhanced Sensory Perception, because that's what it truly is. This external energy has been called many other things. Composer Wilhelm Richard Wagner credited his music to clairvoyance, Tchaikovsky called his creative muse his "guest," while Mozart said his music came from the "divine maker."

Others have credited the subconscious mind for tapping into that power. While that's where a lot of the spiritual information enters, that's not where it happens. Your subconscious mind is like a mailbox waiting for the mailman to fill it.

Then there's the "superconscious." This is the collective spirit conscious. It's the most accurate, but a bit too woo-woo for my liking.

Let's keep it simple.

The Computer and the Internet

Imagine this. You buy a brand new laptop computer and you've just pulled it out of the box and turned it on.

The computer is your basic brain with basic operating systems. Just like a computer runs does its fantastic computations in the background, your subconscious brain runs your operating system: your breathing, heart rate, etc.

In short order, you start saving documents, programs, pictures, etc. on your computer. These get stored in the computer memory, just like your brain stores all your experiences.

So let's say that one day you're stuck on the meaning of a word. Most laptops have a dictionary, but for some reason the word is too technical and your laptop dictionary doesn't have the word.

You're stuck. What do you do?

Here's an idea: how about we go on the Internet and search the World Wide Web? Lo and behold, out of the billions of sites and trillions of pages, we find the definition of the word.

The Internet is a worldwide community of information that is seemingly limitless.

That is the spirit world. Just like we can 'tap into' the Internet, we can also tap into the infinite knowledge of spirits. That's why so many creative geniuses credit this superconscience collective for the information they receive.

Some Rules

I'd estimate that 90 percent of the questions I am asked during a psychic consultation are regarding the future. For some strange reason, a lot of people believe that the future is set in stone. I can assure you that it is not.

A client named Ross came to me many years back for a reading and wanted to know how his career was shaping up. It was in January, and I was happy to inform him that everything was looking good. I felt strongly that he was going to get a major promotion with a matching salary.

He was ecstatic and left very happy.

Later in the year I was in a bookstore and, from behind me, I heard someone say, "You suck!"

I turned around and it was Ross. He was scowling at me. I didn't need my intuition to tell me he wasn't happy. I invited him for coffee to find out what he was ticked off about.

"You were wrong! Totally wrong!" he said. "I was bypassed for the promotion completely."

I was more than stunned. It just didn't make sense. I believed him, but I felt that he was leaving something completely out of the story. I asked him some questions about it, and the truth finally came out.

"Well, there's a situation going on where I apparently harassed a female coworker…"

The story is too long to tell, but it was more than a situation. Ross, a married man, got drunk at a corporate convention and touched a woman inappropriately. Apparently, it was witnessed by many people.

Consequently, the woman threatened to file charges, but later dropped them after he publicly apologized.

Management could have easily fired him. Instead, they retained him, but told him there would be no promotions for a year. He was on probation, so to speak.

He's lucky to still have a job, and lucky the woman didn't press charges.

He altered his trajectory in a moment of stupidity. When you are in a high-profile position, you have to hold yourself to a higher standard. Getting loaded on booze at a conference is not a wise thing. His behavior blackballed him.

The future is never set in stone because we have the human element of free will. All of us are given free will to do or not to do things.

Here's another good example a friend recently shared with me. His wife told him one weekend that the car was making a funny noise and he should get it checked. He chose not to, and on his way to the airport in Phoenix, his car died on the highway. He got a tow truck to get the car, but missed his flight.

He could have easily had the car looked at in time, but he used his free will of choice to not get it checked.

The best way to handle intuitive insights is to see them as a roadmap. You get a good idea of the direction you are going, but there can—and often will—be bumps in the road, along with road closures. Simply adjust your directions and take alternate routes as necessary.

"Watch your attitude," my Mom used to repeatedly say to me in reference to how I perceived things in my young years. "Not everything needs to be labeled 'good' and 'bad,' sometimes it just 'is.'"

We live in Phoenix, Arizona. It's funny to me how people here complain loudly in the summertime when temperature reaches 120 degrees.

"Oh my goodness, I can't believe how hot it is!" they'll complain. "This heat is just terrible!"

You know why it's so hot? It's because it's the desert and it gets crazy hot every single summer and has done so since the early settlers. The heat isn't bad. The heat is heat. Live here and 'yer gonna get hot!

I spoke to another man who got caught in traffic in a cab and missed his flight. He was livid. He discovered shortly after that the flight he missed was hijacked and he would have been one of the casualties of 9/11.

Maybe missing that flight wasn't so bad?

Karma and Blocks

I won't go too deeply into this since it's a bit outside the scope of this book, but it's worth briefly mentioning.

We have all lived before. Many, many lives. So karma plays an important factor in our lives.

Karma is neither good nor bad. Think of it as a teacher giving lessons. In our lives we'll have karmic lessons that we are not meant to know about in advance.

When you hear of psychics talking about "blocks," it's because we are literally being blocked from receiving information about something.

Let go of the expectation that you will "know" everything by being more intuitive. You won't.

I recently visited Todos Santos, Mexico, for a music festival and brainstorming session with my good friend, Geoff. On the last night, I tripped on the cobblestone road and literally smashed my face into the ground, breaking my nose.

You wouldn't believe how much teasing I got.

"Wow, Blair, some psychic you are… didn't you see that coming?"

I laughed it off and replied, "Yes, I did...as I was falling!"

Even though I'm highly intuitive (and will teach you to develop yours to a higher level), I still have accidents, karma, and lessons to learn!

White Light Protection

A lot of people worry unnecessarily about evil spirits, or negative things happening to them when they're connecting with their spirit guides. So let's go back to square one.

When you were created, you were created from spirit, from the source, from God – from whatever you call the highest power. So, you are a being of light. Your spirit guides were assigned to you by the highest power to help you along your physical path and physical journey. So when you think of it logically, the very fact that you're from the light and your guides are from the light, there's absolutely nothing to be afraid of. In fact, there's no sane reason why you shouldn't be listening to your guides.

With that said, I've read a number of books and have heard other spiritual leaders discuss darkness and the dangers. Quite frankly, I'm not at all surprised that people are so frightened by that. But let me explain how your guides can help you eliminate that fear.

Picture a very sharp knife. It can be used carefully and safely to cut various foods. But it can also be unwisely used. You could cut yourself, or cut someone else. The knife itself is neither good nor bad. What matters is how you use it. It's the same with your guides. They are inherently safe. It's how you use them that matters. You don't need to fear the darkness. As many religious texts talk about, light always dispels darkness.

If you're in a dark room and can't see anything, you light up a candle or a flashlight or flick on the lights to see. The light immediately destroys the darkness. That's what it's like with us. We don't need to worry about the evil and darkness because we dispel it through the light within us.

With all of that said, it never hurts to protect yourself with white light. It's almost like double protection to ensure that everything is good. Here is how to do that through a quick and simple meditation:

Close your eyes and imagine you're in a beautiful field.

There are beautiful rolling hills in every direction.

You're in the middle of nowhere. Nobody can bother you. Nobody can get to you.

Now just breathe.

Straight above you are the sky, clouds, and a beautiful white light coming through those clouds and shining down on you like a spotlight.

That white light is so bright, so warm. It feels like you're bathing in it, almost like standing in a shower with it flowing over you. It's an incredibly awesome feeling.

But you're not only surrounded in the white light...it flows inside you. It fills up every single molecule of you. You are flooded with that white light.

You can now choose for that white light to remain with you, or you can turn it off. I'm going to ask you to let it remain with you. I want you to say thank you.

There you go. You're filled with white light. That light dispels the darkness.

Connecting with spirit is completely safe. By surrounding and filling yourself with white light, you've got added protection.

The rule of thumb is this: don't play with fire. I jokingly say in my live events to avoid evil like the plague. Don't conjure up evil spirits and you'll be fine.

I had a discussion with a person recently about things like the Ouija board. Is the Ouija board dangerous? If you're walking down a street and you see a portal to hell, don't open it. I usually say that with a big smile in front of my audiences, and it gets a good laugh from them, because who in his right mind would open a portal to hell? But, if you use things like Ouija boards or anything else to stir up the dark side, then that's your own doing.

So, my advice is simple: don't do that. Fill yourself and surround yourself with white light. Connect with your spirit guides, and all shall be well.

Step One: You Are Psychic

You are psychic.

Yes. You.

Each and every one of us is psychic to a greater or lesser degree. No, you might not be psychic enough to set up shop in your local community as a tarot card reader, but you are psychic.

Each and every one of us has had experiences of déjà vu. We've all felt things were going to happen, and in some cases, they did.

When I was a kid, I used to know who was on the phone before my mom or dad would pick it up. Back then, that was called psychic. Today, it's called Caller ID!

There's nothing unusual about it. In fact, most people readily admit to it.

We all have spirit and guides directing us. So it's natural that we have the ability to sense things, both good and bad, coming our way. It is as natural as breathing.

You don't have to "do" anything to make it work. In fact, it's better to just let it work.

The less you try, the better it is.

I'm not a big fan of jargon, as I prefer to keep everything Zen-like and simple. However, it is worth understanding some of the terminology.

We all have five senses. We see, hear, feel, smell, and taste. In the psychic world, we jazz it up a bit by adding a French flair to it with the word *clair*, which means "clear." A psychic sees things beyond normal senses.

Psychic Definitions

Clairvoyance is the ability to see that which cannot be seen. It is commonly misused to mean all things psychic, but that's not exactly the case. It means, literally, to see things.

Many years ago, my friend's uncle was at the beach enjoying the hot sun. Restless, he got up and walked over to a rocky part of the beach. He was drawn to one particular rock and, upon turning it over, discovered underneath was a drenched fifty-dollar bill.

My friend and other family members hurriedly looked under dozens of rocks but found nothing.

The one and only rock that his uncle was drawn to had the fifty-dollar bill. This example brings up a valuable point: you may not know what you are seeking when you are intuitively drawn to something. In this case, his restlessness drew him to the rocks and to a specific rock in question.

This is clairvoyance – knowing that which cannot be known.

Clairaudience is the psychic ability to hear messages. The messages can come in the form of words or sounds. The voices can be your own internal voice, and sometimes the voice of someone else.

Many religious texts have stories of the voice of God speaking to various people when there was clearly nobody around.

It can also be in the form of sound. Paul McCartney dreamt of the tune "Yesterday." Mozart would hear music in his mind and simply record it. Writers often describe their creative thoughts as their 'muse.' Author Henry Miller suffered from writers block once when, suddenly, his 'muse' woke up. He wrote, "From this moment on—up until four o'clock this morning—I am in the hands of unseen powers. I put the typewriter away and commence to record what is being dictated to me." (Henry Miller, Black Spring, Obelisk Press 1936)

Clairsentience is extremely common. It's simply sensing something without any evidence to support it.

For example, how often have you sensed that something just wasn't right, but you couldn't put your finger on it? Later, you find out that something was wrong, but you couldn't find that trail that led back to you "knowing."

Even though clairsentience is the most common psychic trait we all have, it's the most difficult to explain in words. Simply think of it as knowing without proof.

Clairalience is very cool. It is the psychic sense of smell, except the scent isn't nearby.

When I smell the purple flower heather, I'm often reminded of Scotland or my grandfather. My great uncle used to smoke a pipe and had a custom-made blend of tobacco made for him that had a hint of cherry to it. Although I'm allergic to smoke, I can sometimes pick up on that and know there's a message there for me.

It's important that you don't think when you experience clairalience. It isn't the smell that's the message; it's the bridge to the first thought that will help you most. I will explain this in detail later, but for now, just be aware of scents.

Clairambience is the psychic sense of taste. You might pick up on a taste or flavor as you go about your day. For example, you might pick up the taste of chocolate, mint, or vinegar. It can be sweet, sour, good, or horrible. Whatever the taste is, it will have a bridge to something important.

For example, I remember one day when I was tasting butterscotch. I immediately thought of my dad. He adored butterscotch candy. It brought me an instant wonderful memory of him, as he would often tease my mother by sucking on the candy loudly—something she hated—just for a laugh.

I was recently in a resort and walking down a hall-way when the taste of burnt toast came to me. I was puzzled and didn't know what that meant other than pos-sibly a small fire. Nothing happened while I was there, but a week later in the same resort, a small fire broke out during maintenance and caused smoke damage.

Now you know the terminology.

Now, forget it.

You don't need the fancy terms. All you need is the awareness that you are indeed psychic. Awareness is the key to succeeding in becoming more intuitive and psy-chic. It makes no difference how you get your intuitive messages.

If, for example, a relative wanted to send you ten thousand dollars, would you care if it came by cash, check, bank wire, money order, or direct deposit? No, you'd only care about getting the money. The same thing goes with intuition. Don't get hung up on how you get the message, just be open to receiving it.

It really is simple.

Here's another valuable piece of advice: you won't always get the message right. And that's okay. I've been doing this all my life and I still get my impressions wrong. We are human, and we can interpret things wrong. That's just how life is. But don't discount what you get wrong. Take each situation as a learning experi-ence.

When I tasted the burnt toast, it wasn't immediately apparent that it meant there would be a fire at the resort.

Think about it. When you think of the word *fire* in association with a house or building, you typically think of total devastation, right? Well, I intuitively knew that a massive fire wasn't going to happen. But it simply didn't occur to me that there would be a relatively small fire. While I missed it, the message was still there. And that's a good thing. I don't get down on myself when I miss something, nor should you.

I once went to a friend's house and was enthusiastically greeted at the door by him and his wife. They served an amazing barbeque dinner with wine and a delicious chocolate cake. The evening was filled with laughter, stories of the past, and everyone had a good time.

Except . . . something didn't feel right. The air seemed thick and heavy.

I felt that in spite of the fun, laughs, and camaraderie, they were fighting. In spite of them standing at the door arm in arm as I drove away, I felt it was a show. A week later, my friend confessed to me that he and his wife were arguing right before I had arrived. He said they had a screaming match before I came over and after I left.

They were terrific actors! But my intuition gave it away. I'm sure you can relate. Most of us have experienced this exact scenario.

A Fun Experiment

Here's an experiment you can try with a friend or loved one. Sit down face to face with your friend or loved one, close enough that you're almost touching knees with each other. You'll take turns being a sender and a receiver.

The sender should close his eyes and think back to a memory at any point in his life that was happy, sad, or neutral. Maybe it is a happy time, like a wedding engagement. Or maybe it's a sad time when someone died. It could even be a neutral thought, like waiting for the bus. Senders should try to remain expressionless.

The receiver should wait a moment and try to pick up the emotion. It should come clearly: happy, sad, or neutral. Once the receiver knows what it is, say it. The sender will then validate if it right or wrong. Be prepared for some giggles and laughs. It's a lot of fun to try. Take turns trying a few times.

When doing this, there is an element of body language that comes into play. Gamblers call these body language clues "tells.

After you've tried this a few times with your eyes open, try doing it with your eyes closed. You won't be able to see any tells; instead, you'll only be receiving the impressions. Don't be discouraged if you have some misses. You will miss some, but more often than not, it's not the receiver's fault. It will be due to the sender not being entirely sure of what he or she is sending.

For example, standing around and waiting for a bus is both boring and a bit frustrating. So, while it's a neutral thought, I could be projecting that mildly negative energy and cause my receiver to feel a sad emotion. My receiver would technically get my thought wrong, but it would still be valid. There would be some truth to it. Waiting for the bus is rarely a happy and exciting time!

More Fun

"Don't touch!" my mom would hiss.

"I can't help it, this stuff speaks to me," I replied.

This was followed by an abrupt smack to the back of the head.

We were in an antique shop in Northern Ontario. I don't recall exactly where, but the shop was old and dark, and seemed to be a repository of history to my young mind. Every noun had "old" in front of it. History. Memories.

I love antique shops. I'm not so interested in the antiques themselves, but I feel that many of the items are infused with the energy of the previous owners. Have you ever touched an old object and been taken back to a different time? Imagine what it must have been like back in the day when this item was new?

Have you ever been to a pioneer village and seen a man reenact the town blacksmith, using the tools of the trade from one hundred years ago? Have you ever wondered what it must have been like back then?

Psychometry is a fancy-pants word for the intuitive ability to touch objects and get impressions from them. Psychic flashes. To this day, I can't help but touch items and experience what comes to me.

Here's another fun experiment: the next time you are near an antique store, drop in. Walk around. If possible, touch the antiques. See what comes to you. Of course, there will be no way for you to validate your impressions, but do it anyway.

While there is certainly an element of an active imagination at play, there will also be what I like to call "filler information." And this is most often the key psychic flashes to which you want to pay attention.

A few years ago, I had the opportunity to touch one of Elvis Presley's jumpsuits and belts. Right before touching the sleeve and belt, I anticipated getting a vibration of being on stage with thousands of light bulbs going off. I imagined I'd be hit with the energy and enthusiasm that Elvis was known for putting into his live shows.

For the jumpsuit, I got nothing. Frankly, it was a bit disappointing.

However, the belt buckle gave me a flash of frustration and loneliness. I felt like life was a grind, that I was surrounded by a lot of people but with no true friends. I have to confess, I was a bit stunned. Why? Because that's not what I wanted to feel or experience. I wanted to experience the exciting part of Elvis's life.

But instead of getting his façade, I got his real soul.

Later, however, I felt a deep sense of appreciation for Elvis—the man, his love of his fans, and his love of the music. Unfortunately, like many people of that era, Elvis got caught up in the wrong lifestyle, which eventually led to his downfall.

Developing Your Intuitive Skills

My best advice for developing your intuition is very simple. In fact, most who take my advice discover noticeable leaps in their accuracy and skills within two weeks!

Get yourself a small notebook or journal. I personally love a Moleskine® notebook, which has elastic that holds it shut and a small pocket in the back. It has been around so long that it was used by Ernest Hemingway, Pablo Picasso, and Oscar Wilde.

The system is simple. Every day, write down the impressions or signs you get. Don't judge or over think. Just put them from pen to paper. Do this every day for at least two weeks.

Here's the trick: don't think.

If you get an impression, write it down. Don't go back the next day and review. Just get the impressions, write them down, and forget about them

At the end of the first two weeks, go back and look at what you wrote.

If you are trusting your flashes and writing them down without thinking, you'll likely discover that many of the things either have come true, or you were close in your interpretation. Patterns will emerge.

Keep doing this, and at the end of each week, go back and review.

Here's what will likely happen to you, which happens to most people: your first week will be very weak. However, like a muscle, the more you use it, the stronger it will become. A weightlifter can't hit the gym and lift weights, and then not return for a month and expect to be in shape. It takes consistent effort to improve and get stronger.

Here's why this is so important, by way of an analogy: if I say Los Angeles, Sacramento, Hollywood, Beverly Hills, and Napa Valley, what am I talking about? If you said California, you are absolutely correct. Of course, I didn't actually say "California," but the cities—or the signs—pointed us there, didn't they? It's the same with your natural psychic ability. A single "sign" might not make sense, but several will start to connect like pieces of a puzzle. Keeping a journal to start will really help you see patterns and messages.

Try it. You'll be very surprised at the results. The positive side effect to all of this is that your life will start to improve as you trust your intuition!

Step Two: The Pendulum

Here is a fun way to connect with your spirit guides and develop your personal intuition.

A pendulum is by far the easiest of all divination devices to use. Pendulums go way back in time, but they were most popular in the 1920s when a little string with a ball was sold under the title of "Sex Detector." With this advertised contraption, farmers could determine the sex of unborn animals, even chicks in eggs. Many people have also used, or have heard of using, a string and a paper clip over a pregnant woman's tummy to determine if she is having a boy or girl.

However, a pendulum is much more amazing than that. It can answer questions and help guide you along the way.

Is it evil? Well, Abbé Alexis Mermet was a French Catholic priest who used a pendulum extensively. He called it *radiethesia* and was called the King of the Dowsers in Europe. It's no wonder, as he helped discover water in Africa, and helped find missing bodies of people and a cow that had vanished. Even the Vatican contacted him to find missing documents, which have been recorded in the Archives of Vatican.

If you are not comfortable using one, then don't. But there is, in my opinion, nothing evil about it

Your Own Pendulum

Pendulums are easy to make. The two qualities are simply a string or cord, and a weight at the end. You could use a thread and a needle, but many people find that the needle is not heavy enough. When I demonstrated this in psychic workshops years ago, I simply handed out a six-inch string with a metal nut that I bought from the hardware store. It works.

The best pendulums can be found at new age shops and are relatively inexpensive. My wife has pendulums made for us in small quantities that we bring to Sedona and take into the vortexes there. Sensitive people can feel the energy radiate from them. Check out my website, **www.BlairRobertson.com**, to see if we have them available. They are called "Vortex Pendulums™."

One of my favorite pendulums is a one-inch crystal on the end of a leather cord. It is beautiful and yet simple.

Whatever you finally decide, treat it with respect, and keep it in a safe place when not in use. I recommend storing it in a small bag. Due to their small size, they easily fit into a purse or pocket. Naturally, if you make one that is a necklace, you just put it safely around your neck.

Sit down and hold your pendulum at the end of the cord with the weighted end hanging down. The left hand is considered the psychic hand, so I recommend starting with your left hand. Let the pendulum hang down. I suggest resting your elbow on a tabletop to keep it steady.

Here's a fun experiment that I learned from my friend and psychic author, Richard Webster, in New Zealand: make sure your legs and arms are uncrossed. This is called an open position. Let the pendulum swing naturally. While it is swinging, cross your legs and/or arms and the pendulum will stop swinging.

Isn't that fun? Body language experts tell us that a person with folded arms and legs in the closed position and resistant. This negative energy is picked up by the pendulum

White Light

Before you begin, ask your guides to surround you in white light for protection, as well as for clarity in answers. Keep it simple—your guides know you well, and asking for the white light is free!

"Please surround me in white light protection and help me get to the bottom of this question, please. Thank you!"

Yes or No?

Think of the letter "o" in the word *no*. It is spelled n-o. Well, when the pendulum swings in a circular motion, either clockwise or counter-clockwise, that means the answer is no.

Simple, right?

And for yes, it will swing in a straight line.

See how easy that is? Instead of learning the meanings of seventy-eight Tarot cards, you just learned how to get answers in a few minutes.

But before you do anything, though, you need to calibrate your pendulum.

Calibrate Your Pendulum

Psychics experience "blocks" at times. A block is simply something that is not meant to be known at a certain time or is too obscure.

The pendulum will tell you immediately if it is ready to give you information. We calibrate it by asking a fun question that we know the answer to. My favorite question to start with is, "Am I male or a female?" Allowing the pendulum to dangle down, I will get it swinging in any direction.

I then ask it, "Am I a woman?" I patiently wait and sincerely hope that it starts swinging in a circle!

If it swings in a straight line or stops dead, it means it is not time to ask it questions and I will leave it for a day or so. There is no reason to work with the pendulum if it is going to give you wrong answers. In most cases, though, it will answer correctly and you will be ready to begin.

Please do not skip the calibration step. I've been using pendulums since I was a young child, and over the years when people have complained about it not working, it's because they didn't calibrate it.

Take Your Time

Take your time. Some days when I use my pendulum, it starts quickly and answers questions with a rather violent action. Other times, the pendulum is slow to respond and scarcely moves. I'm not sure why this is; perhaps it's the level of energy around it, but it doesn't matter. Be patient. It is truly an amazing thing.

How to Ask Questions Correctly

Assuming the calibration question was answered correctly, you can go ahead and ask the pendulum questions. The rule for doing that is simple: always ask the pendulum questions that can be answered with a yes, no, or unknown/blocked.

While it is perfectly fine to calibrate it with a fun question, I urge you to ask the pendulum only serious questions. Please don't use it as a toy. With that, some sample questions would be "Should I study harder for the test tomorrow?" or "Is someone stealing food from the refrigerator at the office?"

Don't ask, "Should I take the trip this weekend or not?" because it cannot be answered with a yes or no.

The pendulum will, in all likelihood, stop dead giving you a non-answer. Instead, "Should I take the trip this weekend?" is all you need to ask.

Are We There Yet?

One strong suggestion: don't repeatedly ask a question again and again, hoping for a different answer. There's nothing more annoying than a kid asking, "Are we there yet? Are we there yet?" You don't have to like the answer to the question, or you may be put out by a non-committal block, but when that happens, make sure you give it a rest for a reasonable amount of time.

A Word of Caution

Be careful of asking the pendulum questions that are emotionally charged. For example, "Will I get back together with Bob?" is not a good question to ask after a breakup, especially if the thing you most want is to get back together! It's too emotionally charged. "Will we sell this weekend?" is also a bad question to ask if everything is riding financially on a yes answer.

These are called unintentional blocks. You aren't intending to screw up an answer, but you are too emotionally close to the subject matter. It's the reason why surgeons are not allowed to work on family members. They are too close to the person. If you must find out the answer, ask a friend who is disconnected from the situation to hold the pendulum.

I have also seen, in some cases, where the pendulum can be mischievous, so make sure to calibrate it and ask only serious questions.

One time I was at a college where I gave a demonstration of the pendulum to a bunch of students before an event. Later, the organizers asked me out to a pub for a meal and a beer. At the pub, a couple of tipsy students were asking the pendulum, "Hey, is Fred's penis one inch long. Yes . . . ha, ha, ha!" I clenched my teeth, as this was very disrespectful, but at the same time I chuckled that the pendulum did indeed answer "yes."

Mischievous. At least, I hope it was mischievous!

Free Will

The pendulum may give you an answer that you don't like, or the outcome could change. It is answering the question from the position of "right now" and will show you the most likely outcome.

Remember that you have free will. The pendulum, for example, may answer yes to your question about taking a trip, but you still might choose not to go.

You are not a train on a track that has a predetermined destiny. You have flexibility and choice in your path and direction.

More Questions

Now that you've had some experience with the pendulum with regard to questions to ask, you can advance forward to more detailed ones. It is very helpful, if you are making a decision that has multiple parts, that you ask the questions in a reasonable order. I find it helpful to write the questions on paper and put them in a logical order. Think in steps: what has to happen first, what would be next, etc.

Simply ask the pendulum the first question and then, from that answer, move to the next.

Imagine this. You're thinking of taking a vacation, and while you have a decent amount of money saved, you are not sure if you should blow it all on an expensive one or just use some of it for a local one. It's frustrating you so much that you can't seem to make a decision.

Grab a piece of paper and write down three locations. One is a short distance, the other longer, and the last would require plane fare. No two people work the same way, so there is no right or wrong. If it were me, I'd likely write the three destinations down first, then figure out where we would stay, and finally the date.

"Should I go to Mexico?" is answered "no."

"Should I go to Sedona?" is answered "no."

"Should I go to Palm Springs?" gets a strong "yes!"

From here, I would move on to the location. Maybe a rental home or a hotel? Finally, I'd ask when I should go. Of course, you could ask questions by budget instead. There's no right or wrong. Let the pendulum help you work it out.

A Word About Gambling

My wife and I do a fair amount of business in Las Vegas, Nevada. Wendy loves to play slot machines. With that said, she's very budget conscious and holds very firmly to an allocated amount. On our last trip, she spent $200 on the machines.

I don't understand gambling. I've done it and it is fun for a short while, but I think you're better off just walking up to the pit boss and handing him the $200. That would be a better use of time! Gambling casinos are designed to separate you from your money. But if you can be like Wendy and stick to an affordable budget, then by all means have fun.

However, never use a pendulum, oracles, or go to psychics for gambling purposes. The pendulum will *not* give you winning numbers, and if anything, it will likely give you the wrong information to teach you a lesson. Don't do it.

Fun with The Pendulum

I did say that you should treat the pendulum with reverence and respect. But that doesn't mean you can't have fun with it.

My grandfather taught me an astonishing and tremendously fun game with the pendulum. The purpose was to give me confidence in using it and trusting it to help me, yet for it to be fun at the same time.

One game was called "Find The Murderer." You get together with a bunch of friends in a room. You tell them that a murder is going to take place with a weapon you introduce – something fun – such as a roll of toilet paper. You then leave the room while the group selects the murderer and the murder victim.

When you are called back in, you reveal that you have the world's greatest lie detector, and you show your pendulum. You then ask someone to hold the pendulum and, after showing them what means "yes" and what means "no," you go through the names of those present to find the murderer.

It's absolutely uncanny to your friends and fun to do!

By the way, when you first walk into the room, use your natural intuition. Don't guess, but see if you can sense who the murderer is and who the victim was. For example, if you think Ron was the murderer, start with him first! You will find that as you develop, you'll simply "know" who did what more than half the time.

Another fun game is "Find The Object." Introduce the pendulum to a group of friends. Ask one of them to name any object in the room. Ask the pendulum to point to it. The pendulum will swing *away* from you, and that is where the object is. In other words, pay attention only to the forward swing, not the return swing.

Note: if the object is behind you in either direction, you'll find that the pendulum will swing back and forth.

Simply turn in either direction and it will swing in the proper direction.

For example, say you are facing the group and someone calls out the pink chair which would be at about two o'clock in front of you. Will it, and the pendulum will swing from the two o'clock to the eight o'clock direction. Since you only are interested in the forward swing, the two o'clock direction is correct!

Prepare yourself. Your friends and family will think this is a joke and that you did that on purpose. So, confidently offer to have anyone try it. They will take the pendulum, another object will be called out, and voila! They will be shocked and amazed!

This demonstration never fails to entertain for a long period of time. You might want to have several pendulums available, as all will want to have a try!

Advanced Technique

If you've ever seen or played with a talking board, also known commercially as a "Ouija™ Board," then you'll notice that the letters of the alphabet are arranged in a half-moon manner. Same with the numbers.

By writing such letters and numbers out on a large piece of paper and using the direction method, you can work out names, dates, places, and numbers. Again, it's the forward swing that is the pointer, not the return swing.

This can work very well, although it can be a slow process.

Common sense prevails here, by the way. For example, if you are thinking of taking a trip to Mississippi or Florida, you only need the pendulum to point to the first letter. You'll be there all day long trying to spell out M-I-.S-S-I-S-S-I-P-P-I!

Many people use this technique to discover how many children or grandchildren they will have. In the old days, this was very accurate, but not so much today due to birth control. So, don't be surprised to have the pendulum point to eight children, as that is a "potential" number that may never manifest itself.

How Does This Work, Blair?

I'm often asked if I believe that Spirit guides move the pendulum. My answer is this: no.

Pendulums work by ideomotor response. What this means is that minute muscle twitches cause the pendulum to swing or change direction. That's how it manifests itself.

Many years ago, a man named Michel-Eugène Chevreul studied the pendulum. For twenty years in fact. He believed that it was subconscious movement that caused it to move. Skeptics and non-believers are very quick to point this out, and are often shocked that I am completely in agreement with them!

This is not mysterious in and of itself.

From my experience as a hypnotist, I can tell you that we have two "minds"—the conscious and the subconscious. The conscious is limited. The subconscious? It is in your subconscious that Spirit works. It is in your subconscious that your karmic records are accessed. It is your subconscious that solves problems while you sleep.

The subconscious is powerful. Don't believe me? Well, let me ask you this: how much concentration did you exert in the past five minutes to make your heart beat? Or to breathe in and out? That's right. Zero. You made absolutely *no* conscious effort to breathe or to make your heart beat. But you are alive because your subconscious is taking care of you!

How often have you gone to bed with a problem and awoken with a solution? Many people have experienced this. It happened to Thomas Edison regularly, and Albert Einstein "invented" the theory of relativity as the result of a dream.

The universal power is omnipotent. It has access to use whatever it needs at its disposal to deliver messages. The universal mind delivers the messages. Period. Don't let anyone dissuade you from using a pendulum.

Have Fun!

In my short lifetime, I have found pendulums to be invaluable tools to validate what my guides are trying to show or teach me. I have a drawer full of beautiful pendulums that have been given to me from friends and family, including two very special ones: one given to me by my daughter, Beth, and one by my wife, Wendy.

Pendulums have helped me along my path, and in my constant desire to simplify life, I have found them to be one of the greatest and easiest divination tools to use.

Please use your pendulum for good, and I look forward to hearing about your success!

Step Three: Numerology

I love numerology and I love teaching it. Even if you hate math like I do, it's super easy to do and it reveals a lot about a person's personality.

In this fun exercise, we are going to discover a person's life path number. This is considered one of the most important numbers in numerology. When I taught this in my Intuitive Edge Workshop, I learned very quickly that it was hard to regain the group's attention because once you learn it, they would start doing calculations for their friends, family, loved ones, and people they work with.

The life path number reveals their main strengths and weaknesses.

Want a fun way to discover if you are a young or old soul karmic-wise? You can do this quite easily with numerology. It's so fun and easy to do.

Technically, it can be argued that you don't need to use any intuition to do numerology, and this is true for the most part. However, intuition gives us a baseline to start with. When you know a child's strengths and weaknesses, you can help direct that child better in life.

Knowing this information can help you to foretell things that are likely to come up, how a person will likely handle situations, etc. So, don't leave your intuition out of the mix!

Okay. Let's have some fun!

All you need is a pencil and paper. Simply add your birth year plus your birth month and birth date together. For example, let's say Janice is born on April 5, 1977. April is the fourth month, so we add (4+5)+1977, which gives us a total of 1986. Next, we add those numbers together, so we add 1+9+8+6, which gives us twenty-four.

Numerology Rule

The rule is that we must keep reducing the number down to a single digit, except if the result is an eleven or twenty-two. These are called master numbers, which I'll explain in a moment.

Twenty-four is not a master number, so we add the 2+4, and that gives us a number of six. In numerology we call this a "life path" number. Janice has a life path number of six.

To determine if someone is a young soul or old soul, we look at this number. The lower the number, the younger the soul. Obviously, the higher the number, the older the soul.

To put it another way, the bigger the number, the more lifetimes you have had.

Again, I'd like to point out that while you might be a wise, old soul, that can also mean challenges will be given to you that wouldn't even be considered for a young soul!

One trait I have found that old souls get challenged on is patience. It seems old souls are constantly having things put in their lives to test patience. For example, I'm an old soul (my master number is 22) and I have to say that I'm as impatient as you can get.

Contrarily, young souls tend to rush into things without thinking, and end up making a mess of situations.

No matter what you are, there will be things to learn. But no matter what, the faster you can learn and master these things, the greater your life will be!

Now that you've read this far, I'm sure you would like to know a little bit about yourself and your life path number. Here are the basic meanings.

Life Path Numbers

Life Path Number One: People with a life path number one are young souls. They are new around here!

Ones tend to start off life dependent and may be slow starters in life. But just like a child is dependent on parents from a young age, this shouldn't be construed as a negative trait. In fact, as they mature, they become more and more independent.

Curiously, they tend to end up in the number "one" position: they often start businesses, reach high levels in work-related activities, make great sales people, etc.

Their life challenge is to avoid being selfish and self-centered. Ones tend to be very charming and persuasive. Ones can be very stubborn and inflexible, which helps them achieve their desires most of the time, but it can equally be their downfall.

Ones must be wary of rushing things, as doing so almost always ends up in a roadblock.

Honesty and loyalty tend to be words you hear about these folks.

Life Path Number Two: People with a life path number two are givers in life, tending to look after everyone else first and themselves second. Rarely do they take the lead role.

They prefer to be invisible and in the background.

Think of a president or prime minister giving a perfect speech or answering questions in a brilliant manner. What many don't realize is that it's the staff behind the scenes that brief the "number one" and make him or her look great without sharing in the limelight. This is the number two's role to perfection.

Twos are powerfully persuasive and diplomatic in a soft, gentle manner. Most people won't realize that they have been influenced by a two until it's too late!

They tend to be sensitive, often to a negative degree. This lifetime will be a test to learn to value themselves and their contributions. Twos are very intuitive due to their sensitivity.

Twos make excellent and trustworthy friends.

Life Path Number Three: People with a life path number three are often multi-talented and highly creative people.

Threes are great conversationalists but often you can't get them to be quiet. They have a strong underlying need to communicate through speech, the written word, or through the arts.

This lifetime is all about enjoying life. They are often found busy having fun.

Threes tend to skim over things. They don't want a lot of detail, which can often be their downfall, as they tend to not like to have to do things that could cause them frustration.

In early life, threes tend to be moody and hard to please. This changes, though, as they realize that they can use their charm and wit to get things more in line with how they want them to be.

Threes have amazing imaginations and are problem solvers. What most people find challenging, they tend to see right through. Threes are very valuable in business in creating breakthroughs and thinking outside the box. When questioned about their ideas, they'll likely state that these ideas were "obvious," leaving the rest befuddled.

Threes tend to excel in communications, like teaching and in entertainment. They need a lot of variety to be happy in life.

Life Path Number Four: People with a life path number of four are masters at creating order out of chaos.

They are typically very slow-moving and methodical. They dot every "I" and cross every "T."

Fours are hardworking, honest, and loyal. They tend to come across to others as rigid and stiff.

Fours get the job done, but in this lifetime, they need to appreciate themselves and reward themselves on a regular basis. If they do not, this can lead to a life of quiet desperation, which is not good.

Fours don't handle instability very well. In today's day and age, it is a life lesson to which they must adjust.

The faster that they can achieve modest financial independence, the better off they will be.

Parents of fours would do well to teach them to save and plan early on to help them along the way.

Fours can do almost any job and excel when left alone.

Fours can take time to settle down in love, but when they do they tend to mate for life and are tremendous lovers.

Around mid-life, they tend to shift focus toward helping others and can often be found doing much for charity.

Life Path Number Five: People with a life path number five have experienced enough previous lives to understand working hard and playing hard.

Fives tend to sort out their strengths and weaknesses early in childhood, and as they mature, they tend to work toward their strong points.

Fives are restless and very impatient. They must learn in this lifetime to relax, as they can tend to get stressed out, sometimes dangerously so.

Fives will have a childlike attitude throughout life. They tend to never really grow up and are often the life of any party or gathering.

Distraction and lack of focus in the first half of their life has the potential to cause problems with jobs and settling down in relationships. The earlier they learn to focus and control their interest, the happier they will be.

With that said, fives tend to roll with things very well, even if they fall apart.

Because fives know their strengths, they can be counted on to do a great job in whatever it is that they do. They take pride in their accomplishments. They are contagious with enthusiasm and are great for building a "we can do it" attitude.

It seems like fives have it all to an unfair degree. And to a degree they do. One major area of concern, though, is that of overindulgence in food, booze, or drugs. Balance is key, or they can often bring misery to themselves.

Fives are fun to be around and highly generous. Success in virtually anything tackled is common.

Life Path Number Six: People with a life path number six can be described by the words *comfort, love, care,* and *assistance.*

Sixes make great doctors, nurses, and caregivers. Virtually anything in the service of others, they will excel at to an incredible degree.

Family is very important to sixes. In many ways, it is their life. In this lifetime, they understand the value of a close family and will go to the ends of the earth to maintain balance, harmony, and discipline.

Sixes see things clearly, are excellent negotiators, and amazing at diffusing difficult situations.

Without question, sixes are the least selfish in this lifetime. While they do value and highly appreciate material things, don't be confused—sixes can be very wealthy in this lifetime, but their wealth will be directly attributed to a return for the amount of selfless love and caring they give.

Another trait that stands out for sixes is fairness. They recognize that they cannot please everyone, but they are both confident and fair when it comes to judgment. As such, they make great judges and make fair decisions.

Life Path Number Seven: People with a life path number seven have achieved and learned much from past lives regarding materialism and related lessons. This time through will find them being much more spiritual, loving, and giving.

They are often great with details and usually have a keen interest in technology.

Sevens can tend to be awkward and shy in their early years, and if they don't push outside of their comfort zone, they risk being like that their whole lives. That would be a shame because these people are both fascinating and inspiring.

Sevens, due to their ability to get to the bottom of things, are excellent thinkers, analysts, and programmers.

They are able to easily tap into a vast spiritual database of solutions. Their solutions can often seem magical.

Sevens must learn to control their tempers and not allow themselves to get upset. Just because they have a spiritual nature does not mean others will understand them, so one must learn to be at peace with that.

While some might consider them loners, they are true friends once you get to know them on a deep level.

Life Path Number Eight: People with a life path number eight are magnets for success and achievement, although not necessarily in their youth or even early years.

Eights tend to jump in with both feet and tackle large-scale tasks often with startling results.

Donald Trump encourages people to "think big." Eights are the big thinkers and expect compensation when the goals are achieved.

Eights must learn in this lifetime to share. We need eights, as they drive the economy and create jobs, but they can tend to focus only on themselves. Eights who master the balance of sharing their success are aligned to achieve even greater success and are often tremendous leaders.

However, if they fail to learn this lesson, they run the risk of crashing and having to start all over again.

Life Path Number Nine: People with a life path number of nine are humanitarians. They are here to learn to care for others and the earth.

Because of their sensitivity, they are tremendous lovers and givers. They tend to be easily hurt by others and must learn in this lifetime to seek to understand.

Unfortunately, in their effort to help and give, they can often run the risk of being taken advantage of by others, even family.

The hardest part for them to learn in this lifetime is the difference between helping and enabling.

A deep love for the simple things in life, they make cheap dates: romance to them is just being together under the stars or for a walk along the beach. They value and cherish everything in life and are sentimental.

Life Path Master Number Eleven: People with a life path number of eleven are old souls. They have lived many, many lives before. They have experienced great joys and terrible tragedies, and this lifetime is one of balance.

Extremely capable of virtually anything they attempt, elevens can tend to be dreamers and barely achieve a fraction of what they are capable of early in life. This is often frustrating to them, as it is like having a warehouse of capability but without an open door to access it.

This tends to change later in life, with them understanding their capabilities and becoming determined to put all their efforts into achievement.

Elevens tend to be nervous and under a great deal of pressure, both externally and internally. While younger, they tend to not live to their potential, but as they get older, they can suffer from the feeling of never being good enough. This can cause problems if they don't seek balance.

Elevens must learn in this lifetime to set benchmarks and force themselves to be happy when they reach them. This helps them evolve spiritually and brings them happiness and contentment.

Life Path Master Number Twenty-Two: People with a life path number twenty-two are the oldest of souls.

Twenty-twos have all of the strengths and life lessons of all numbers that have gone before them. They are the most evolved. That's the great news.

The bad news is that they have all the potential weaknesses of all the other numbers as well.

Being a numerology step up from eleven means that twenty-twos are capable and practical. They are able to act on plans, take action, and really make things happen.

They are often charismatic and typically end up in leadership positions.

They often excel in multiple areas. For example, they may lean heavily toward being a humanitarian and have the desire to further a worthy cause. This desire, combined with a materialistic ability to generate tremendous money, could mean unbelievable success for the charity. Bill Gates would be an example of this, as he is a twenty-two.

These people tend to be very talented, and when they put their minds to work, they can be very prolific in whatever output they are trying to achieve.

Nervousness is high for them, and like the elevens, twenty-twos must look after their health. Stress often holds them back early in life, but they manage it better later in life.

One life lesson they must learn is to take breaks. They tend to be workaholics and not understand how to holiday or relax.

Almost all twenty-twos do not see measurable success until their mid-forties. About half will simply drift through life before they have an awakening: it can literally be an epiphany that changes them. The other half does well but don't hit that magic combination.

It does happen, though, and when success comes, it typically comes so fast it can make their heads spin!

Try It!

Try working out life path numbers for yourself and your family. It's fun to do and you'll be amazed at the results.

Try looking back at the past few months in your mind and "see" how your number influenced you. Look ahead and "see" how it's affecting your immediate future and the insights in can give you.

Remember, the rule of thumb is that the younger the soul, the more lessons they must learn. In many ways, life will be easier. The older the soul, the greater the potential, but life can bring more challenges and lessons.

All in all, it's great to be alive and learning, don't you agree?

BONUS: Time Projected Empathy: Predicting the Future

Flashback...

In an effort to promote struggling ticket sales for an evening of hypnosis at a venue in Ottawa, Ontario, my friend, Eddie Diijon, suggested adding a "spook show" element and doing a publicity stunt with the local press.

I was well versed in magic history. Midnight ghost shows were the rage from around the 1940s to the 1960s. In 1929, a gentleman named Elwin Charles Peck created a brilliant money-making business concept. He proposed to movie theatres that they open up for a one-night "spook show" to be held at the bewitching hour of midnight. The bottom line was that it was a glorified magic show and a scary movie. Right after the magic show, there would be a "blackout," where ghosts would fly through the air and a wide variety of horrors would occur.

For young gentlemen, it was a huge hit, as their dates would often jump into their arms in sheer fear, and I suspect that during the blackout, other shenanigans took place in the romantic department!

After the blackout, a scary movie would start.

From a business standpoint, theaters made *huge* grosses, as back in those days it wasn't uncommon for a theater to have 1,200 seats. El-Wyn's Midnight Spook Party was a huge hit and spawned thousands of copycats.

Diijon told me to do a "séance" in which I would read for the audience, then finish with a demonstration known among spiritualists as "table tilting." This, he said, would make a great story for the local media.

I was scared stiff, but I took Diijon's advice. Boldly, I called up the two local newspapers. The first newspaper turned me down completely. The second newspaper, *The Ottawa Sun*, invited me to come down for an interview.

From my perspective, the interview didn't go well. The editor said she wanted something more than just an everyday commonplace story. I was naïve. At the time, I didn't realize that she was on my side. She wasn't calling me a fake, but indirectly challenging me to prove my ability.

The Canadian election was coming up, so the editor asked me, "Who is going to win?"

I was stunned. This had nothing to do with hypnosis, a séance, or anything else, but clearly she was locked onto the psychic side.

I said, "Fine. I'll make a prediction." Bravely, I figured regardless if it proved true or not, I'd at least get a line or two in the newspaper.

"What's your prediction?" the editor asked. Thinking quickly back to the vaudeville days, I decided to do something more dramatic.

"Let me make the prediction. Let's seal it in an envelope and you can keep it in a drawer until the day of the election."

She immediately lit up! "What if we seal it in our safe, and we won't touch it until the day after the results are in? We are *insanely* busy the day of the election, so are you good with the following day?"

What the hell was I going to say? No?

Duh.

"Of course! And maybe you could run a contest to see who comes close to the psychic?"

To my absolute shock, she agreed!

We scrambled up some paper, an envelope, and a lock-box. It was locked and held in the Ottawa Sun office safe. Photographers were present while I wrote the prediction.

It is important to point out that historically, Conservative Prime Minister Kim Campbell by far was in the lead. Jean Chrétien was behind. "Liberals" in Canada are left-leaning and "Conservatives" are right-leaning. This is for historical reference – my predictions have never been political in and themselves.

When I wrote my prediction, I paused.

Funny. I didn't really care what the outcome was, but I felt an overwhelming feeling of this being an historical event. I was confused. History, to me, had already been made. Kim Campbell was the first Canadian Prime Minister. If she was to be remembered for anything, though, she was known for passing the "no means no" rape law.

I was confused because, like her or not, she had already achieved a lot

That feeling was pervasive. I didn't understand. However, like most premonitions, your job is not to think—it's to go with what you are feeling. I went ahead with my prediction.

The next day, I got a full-page story about me and my prediction. It promoted my event, and my phone rang non-stop with offers for shows and asking me for readings.

I was stunned.

My first-ever full-page story.

Time passed. Against what I thought was logical, the Kim Campbell Conservatives slid in the polls. However, just like a horse race, some will lead and then trail. It seemed a shoe-in that the Conservatives would win.

Then it happened. Canadians tuned into their televisions and watched as the Kim Campbell Conservatives made fun of Liberal leader Jean Chrétien's face (Chrétien had suffered Bells Palsy as a young boy and the left side of his face is partially paralyzed as a result). The media and public backlash was swift. Both parties were appalled by the ad, and reportedly Prime Minister Kim Campbell disavowed knowing about it.

But it was too late.

On October 25, 1993, there was a Liberal landslide with the Liberals winning 177 seats in the election. The following day, I was ushered into a boardroom by a dozen reporters and photographers. Skeptically, they would not let me anywhere near the box. I stood at one end of the boardroom while, at the other end, they opened my sealed case.

My prediction read: "October 7, 1993, I predict on this day that on October 25 the Conservatives will be no longer and the Liberals will have a majority. I believe they will have 178 seats."

They were stunned.

I have a confession to make. Eddie Diijon encouraged me since the day I met him to be dramatic and "over-the-top." News is, in general, boring. Diijon taught me to be dramatic.

I felt the Liberals would win. Even though it seemed impossible at the time, that was my gut feeling and I went with it. I'm glad I did!

In a moment of theatrics, I dramatically wrote, "the Conservatives will be no longer."

Rationally, I was thinking, well . . . if they get beat, they'll be no longer. Doesn't that sound mysterious and impressive? Well, little did I know that the Canadian electorate would *obliterate them*!

The Conservatives went from 156 seats to – get this – two seats! The conservatives were obliterated! It was one of the biggest defeats in Canadian history. To say that this stunned Canadians would be an understatement.

The initial count was 177 seats. However, after a recount, it was deemed that the Liberals would indeed have 178 seats.

Regardless of political affiliation, it was a stunning victory.

The resulting publicity garnered me a full house at my show and media coverage across Canada. To be honest, I wasn't ready for that level of success at that time, but nevertheless, it came!

I was a regular guest from that point on across news media in Canada for my political predictions on local, regional, and national events. I quickly became the media's go-to guy for psychic predictions. I remember many-a-time being awoken by some media outlet wanting information on their local candidate's potential, not caring what time zone I lived in at the time.

Time Projected Empathy

I'm often asked by the media and followers how I do what I do. I call what I do "Time Projected Empathy." Time Projected Empathy is a fancy way of saying what I call "precognition."

The problem I have with that term is that it implies that what is about to happen *will* happen.

This is simply not true. The future is *not* set in stone.

Think about it.

If I were to tell you that tomorrow you would be violently mugged, would you leave your house? Normal people would respond with an aggressive, "No way!" Tomorrow night you'd likely be phoning me up saying, "You aren't a very good psychic, I didn't get mugged!"

So, here's the question. Was I wrong or did *you* change *your* future? From my standpoint, the future is never set in stone. If you are "supposed" to get mugged tomorrow and alter your path, then you've changed your future!

Take any legend in history. Elvis Presley, for example. *If* he had not taken those drugs, would he have died? *If* Buddy Holly or Big Bopper had not gotten on that plane, would they have died? Whitney Houston. Michael Jackson. The list goes on.

The bottom line is that we will never know. They did. And they died. It was their time, clearly. But one must wonder, right?

Every Sunday night, almost without exception, I go for a walk and wind down. Typically, my wife, Wendy, goes to bed. I head into my office and light candles. It's something I've done since I was a kid. I almost always light incense. If the weather is nice, I open the patio door that is adjacent to my office and allow the warm Arizona breeze to blow in.

On my desk I have a replica of the late, great, Jeane Dixon's crystal ball pedestal, and I have my own crystal ball. I get out a Moleskine ™ notebook and I use a Mont Blanc™ fountain pen for writing.

I clear my mind.

What happens next is often very uncanny.

What I do is available to every single one of us. It's difficult to describe, but amazing in nature: I "throw" myself into the future.

What I visualize is an old-fashioned newspaper. There are two ways to read a paper. First, you can read it word for word from front to back. Or you can skim a paper for the headlines. What I do is imagine that I am reading a newspaper in the future. As I skim over the headlines, certain ones jump out at me. From here, I make my predictions and of which—modesty aside—I've become well known for!

For example, I predicted the Space Shuttle explosion, the Ronald Reagan assassination attempt, Pope John Paul II's assassination attempt. I've also predicted the plane crash that killed Polish President Lech Kaczynsk and many members of his cabinet, the death of Michael Jackson, the passing of Whitney Houston, the earthquakes that decimated New Zealand, and the unbelievable earthquakes and tsunami that devastated Japan.

How Does It Work?

In the early days it didn't work all the time. In fact, even to this day, it doesn't work perfectly. It is like a slow-moving bell-curve that causes it to succeed.

On a Sunday night, I'll often get ten or fifteen different impressions. Many are not clear enough for my liking. Remember, newspaper headlines aren't proper sentences. They are short and typically three to four words long. For example, "Mayor approves tax increase," "WIN" (with a picture of local hockey team winning the playoffs), "Explosion kills four," "Dow up record 200 points." You get the idea. They are short and pithy headlines. Some give a complete picture, while others are vague.

When I make formal predictions, I like them to be as specific as they possibly can be. As an example, last Sunday I got an impression of students shooting another student. Unfortunately, that doesn't fit my criteria of being reasonably specific, and I didn't get a time frame for it. In other words, where was the shooting to take place, and when? I had no idea. And it was frustrating, as two days later, three kids in Texas shot a young man because they were bored. When I heard the news, I immediately recognized it, but the feeling was too unclear at the time I first got the impression.

So, out of the ten or fifteen impressions I get, I typically publish the four that are the clearest to me. Do they all prove true? No, of course not. Once again, free will is in play, and the future is never set in stone. Add to this the human factor, and the reality is that sometimes I misinterpret the headlines.

However, a good number of them do prove true, or very close.

Now, what about timelines? How do I get specific with those?

I have to confess that I have yet to be able to express in words exactly how I do this. It's partly a knack and partly art form. It's mostly an intuitive feeling that I can best express as being either "close" or "far." If it feels close, it's going to happen soon. Naturally, if it's far, it will have a further time range.

In the example I gave earlier of the cities, telling you what state I was talking about—California—there are also clues which can give away timelines. Some are obvious: hurricanes tend to happen during hurricane season, snowstorms in the winter, elections during election times. Other times, the headline gives me the information. If I see the headline "Texas gets freak snow" and it's summertime and I feel it is very close, then I can safely predict that there's going to be an unusual snow outbreak.

Blair's Rules for Premonitions

Predictions need to describe what is going to happen and have a reasonable time frame for them to occur. They should be published. "Published" simply would mean writing it down in a journal, or telling a family member or friend. In other words, it's out there to be measured.

When coming up with premonitions, don't force them. That's key. If you force a premonition, you are highly likely to see it fail. Why? Because ego is getting in the way. It doesn't matter what you want, let the "future-facts" speak for themselves. You won't always get timelines, for example. That's fine. Write the premonition down anyway. Whatever you do, don't fall into the trap of believing vague predictions that you have created or that other tabloid psychics create. You know them:

There will be a shooting this year!

There will be a major earthquake this year!

There will be political unrest!

You have to be specific to be terrific. Earthquakes happen all the time, elderly celebrities pass routinely, and there's always political unrest. In order to be an effective prognosticator, there are three things you must do:

First – What is supposed to happen? Describe it.

Second – In what time frame is this supposed to happen? The more specific, the better. Seven days? Thirty days? In the summer? Pinpoint it, or it's vague.

Third – It has to be "published."

Some of the predictions will be misses. In the case of a major catastrophic event, nobody is happier than me when this happens. I don't want earthquakes to happen where they can hurt people.

Other times you'll be off, but close.

I predicted that the 2011, 8.9 magnitude earthquake and tsunami in Japan would happen. I was off by one day. Earthquakes happen all the time in Japan. Tsunamis are frequent there as well. But I "saw" a headline that read "Massive earthquake hits Japan!" I knew it was going to be big, and I knew it would be close. I could feel it.

Don't Shoot The Messenger!

Many people were upset at the Japan prediction. I was flooded with questions like, "Why didn't you try to warn people?"

When I first started, I didn't know how to handle this. I used to feel terrible when these things would happen as though somehow I caused them to happen. I liken the predictions to being like the weatherman. When a weatherman forecasts a possible tornado for tomorrow, he doesn't want that to happen, does he? When it does happen, the weatherman doesn't (or shouldn't) suffer guilt for it. He's just doing his job.

It's the same with predictions that are tragic in nature. I don't want them to happen, but I "report" them.

It takes guts to do this. Trust me, I know. You're sticking your neck out by making a prediction like this. When it proves true, it's powerful, but when you are wrong—or off—then you'll have negative feelings. If you told others, they might even mock you.

Ignore the negativity. Avoid it at all costs and keep trying.

Avoid Negativity

It is inevitable that you will meet up with negativity regarding premonitions. If you wish to develop your intuition, I strongly urge you to avoid people who are negative.

You'll come across two types.

The first will be the obnoxious skeptic. Everything is fake or is a coincidence to them. Just avoid them altogether. You'll never convince them, so don't bother. It's like trying to convert someone from an opposing political point of view to the other side—it's a waste of time and energy. These people are just downright negative.

The second are people who are simply skeptical or perhaps just negative in their outlook on life. Seemingly harmless, their negativity can stack on you like straw on a camel's back. Shake it off. Find someone supportive. I have found the best way to do it is to just say you are trying an experiment. I've done this for years, and in many ways that's exactly what my predictions are—experimentation.

It's very important, especially in the beginning, to not be hard on yourself. You absolutely will misinterpret things and feelings. That's why you need to keep a journal. Jot down your impressions. Throw yourself into the future and report what you see in your journal. After a few weeks go by and you pull your journal out, here's what you'll find:

1. You had hits. Congratulate yourself and thank Spirit.

2. You had absolute misses. Who cares?

3. You had close calls.

Review your close calls. Oftentimes you'll find that what you saw was accurate, but you misinterpreted something small that threw you off course. Don't beat yourself up. It's a learning experience. I'm still learning myself.

I recently told friends that I predicted a plane crash, but was confused about the details. What I saw was a person inside and outside of the plane. I felt it was a bi-plane, but again, it was confusing to say the least. What never occurred to me was that at air shows, "wing walkers" stand on top of the upper wing of the bi-plane. Tragically, one crashed a few days later, killing the pilot and the wing-walker.

Not everything will be clear. And, like the example of the wing-walker, you might not "get" what the message truly is. It doesn't matter. Forge ahead anyway.

Time Projected Empathy is fun, and I hope you'll try it. I predict that you'll enjoy it!

Conclusion

Now that you've completed this book, I urge you to pick just one thing and just start with that.

Perhaps the pendulum will resonate with you.

Numerology might be your thing.

Maybe you're advanced and wish to try my Time Projected Empathy…

Doesn't matter. Just pick one and go for it.

Whatever you do, have fun. Life is meant to be fun.

Live your life to the fullest and blessings to you!

FREE White Light Meditation Audio Download

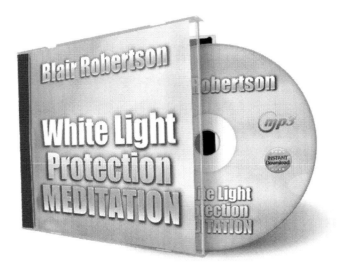

If you would like a FREE white light meditation downloadable audio recorded by author Blair Robertson designed to easily and effortlessly help protect you, then please visit

http://www.BlairRobertson.com/PsychicBonus

About The Author

Blair Robertson is a world-renowned psychic medium dedicated to demonstrating that love never dies, and that Spirit is all around us. Based in Phoenix, Arizona, he lives with his wife Wendy, the love of his life.

Blair has been featured on the Discovery Channel, Fox News, NBC, ABC, and hundreds of radio shows worldwide. He has produced a number of CDs, DVDs, and free online seminars on spiritual subjects.

Blair Robertson tours widely, giving demonstrations of communication with the afterlife. He was once branded a "comedium" by one of his fans for his sense of humor and compassion. Blair excels in delivering messages of love in a loving way.

He has a weekly inspirational newsletter, and we invite you to visit and subscribe at **http://www.BlairRobertson.com**

Free Sample Chapter From Spirit Guides

Step One: Understanding the Five Signs of Communication

Spirit uses the five senses to communicate with us. You've probably heard a lot of people say that psychics have a sixth sense. That's completely untrue. No psychic has sixth sense. Nobody has a sixth sense. We only have five senses.

You've may have heard of what psychics refer to as "Clairs." Clairvoyant, Clairsentient, etc. Claire is a French word that literally just means "clear." So what our guides will do is use our senses that we already have and heighten them so that we can get better use out of them.

What are the five senses that we have? Seeing, hearing, smelling, tasting and touching.

Your guides will communicate with you using sight by having you see a newspaper or a billboard or something on television. You might see a scenario, or a person that will remind you of something. These are visuals that will bring you to something.

For example, my wife and I have hummingbird feeders outside of our home office. My wife loves hummingbird feeders. Hummingbirds coming around all the time. Just recently, before I sat down to put this book together, a hummingbird came by and flew outside of my window. It reminded me of a hummingbird feeder that my mother used to have outside of her window at a cottage that my parents used to own. That in turn made me think of a conversation that I had with my mother 25 years ago that had a message for me. In other words, the hummingbird brought the memory, which brought the memory of my mother, which brought the memory of the conversation I was having just out of the blue that put it all together for me. That's how it works. It's beautiful.

So, in this particular case, I saw something which started the domino effect of one thing leading to another.

You may also hear something that could trigger a message – a particular sound or noise. But here's the trick: you may hear a real sound, or you may think you're hearing a sound. You could hear something like the sound of a person's voice from the past. It could be something as simple as your first grade teacher who said something. Or, as I just mentioned, my high school teacher who always talked about paralysis by analysis.

Smells can also be signs. It could be walking past flowers, or a scent such a perfume or a cigar.

My Great Uncle Kay smoked a pipe with a custom blend of cherry tobacco. He took quite a shine to me when I was a kid and taught me several cool magic tricks that I used to impress my first grade classmates. He encouraged me to step out of my shell and was very patient with me. While I'm a non-smoker, I can still smell that unique aroma, and it's often when I'm lacking confidence. It's my spirit guides encouraging me.

You can get messages through touching things.

Have you ever held an antique that has taken you back in time, so to speak? While much of this is nostalgic and imagination, there are times when you will touch something of significance and you'll simply 'know' that your guides are giving you a message.

Earlier this year I was thinking of a friend of mine in Australia. I'd been thinking of him on and off for a few days and made a mental note to reply to his last letter.

Days went by and I finally pulled out the letter. Upon touching the letter and uncomfortable feeling came over me. I felt an urgency that is hard to put into words. Rather than write him, I decided to phone him.

I got hold of his wife who had just that morning had my friend admitted to hospital and would soon be diagnosed with pancreatic cancer, and died not long after.

It was the touch of the letter and the energy contained that my guides used to alert me that something was wrong.

Had I had written him back—or emailed him—I wouldn't have had a last chance to chat to him, which I got, thanks to my spirit guides.

Tasting is another way to receive signs.

Not as common as the other forms of signs, you can often get messages from taste as well. My mother was a wonderful woman but a horrendous cook. She made the world's most bland food. But every so often when I taste bland food—or simply think of it—there is a message of something that she taught me. I consider this to be an indirect way of communicating, yet still powerful.

The bottom line is this: be open to everything. It could be a song on the radio or a television show. It could be words on a page. It could be something like a scent of a cigar or perfume of some sort. It could be a bumper sticker or one of those vanity plates on a car. It could be anything. Just be open to the signs and let the signs flow. Don't judge them. They—the spirit guides – will create ways for you to piece the puzzle together.

Let's do a quick recap. You may see something this morning at work and it won't have any impact on you. Somebody might say something to you in the middle of the day at work or at lunch time, or something might happen – suddenly, all of the pieces will start to come together. You will get that "ah-ha" moment. That is one of the main ways that your spirit guides will communicate with you.

There is one more thing that I need to teach you, and it's outside of the five signs: your guides are able to connect with you while you're sleeping. So, there's a difference between sleeping and having dreams. When you have a dream, a dream is typically really unusual or weird. The example I like to give is an actual dream that

I had one time. I imagined or dreamt that I got out of bed—I had to go to work and I jumped on a big giant rubber ducky and I floated down a stream which was in place of my street. Of course, you wake up and you think, "Wow, what was that all about?"

Here's the thing to remember: dreams are usually weird and often nonsensical. You'll see people in dreams, like a postman, but one of the signs that you're dreaming is that you usually can't describe the person. You know it's the postman, you know it's a male, but you can't remember their face when you wake up. That's how dreams work. They're not scary people when you see them, they're just sort of blank. You just know the role they're in or who they are or what they are, but typically you're not able to see them. However, while you're sleeping, before you're dreaming, is usually when the connections will come through.

The connections are going to be very, very strong. The connections are going to be very, very clear. You will see things and know things, and everything will be extremely clear to you in such a way that there will be no doubt what it is. That's how your guides can make a connection with you and bring messages to you. It will all be very, very clear.

The messages from our guides will often be so clear that we will know we have to move or have to make a phone call or do something else. In many, many ways, they're able to communicate with us. It will be a message delivered and message received. You will know it when you wake up – if you're aware of it.

Now that you know the five signs of communication and are open to them, let's move to the next step: Quieting Your Mind.

Order Spirit Guides Today: **http://amzn.to/1z0rNTL**

93637556R00048

Made in the USA
Columbia, SC
16 April 2018